From Darkness into Light

story:
Jennifer Degenhardt

illustrator:
Juliette Chattaway

This story is for all who experience challenges with their mental health.
May you find your ray of sunshine.

AUTHOR'S NOTE

Hello!

Thank you for taking the time to read this message before you start reading. It's important that you know what you might find in the pages so you can make a reasonable choice whether or not to dive in.

This story deals with inner turmoil and associated dark thoughts, up to and including those of self-harm. I did not write this story to be triggering to anyone, but rather - as always - to provide an opportunity for discussion. It is my hope that by sharing a story that is based on feelings that I have had personally, that I can help with the discussion about self-harm, suicidal thoughts and the spiral that the human mind can get itself into. Yes, you read that right: I have struggled with depression and delicate mental health for many years, which ultimately led to some really negative thinking. While it is not a time in my life that I wish to revisit, I am grateful for the experience, as it has changed the way I view everything in life.

The first and best thing I did was to ask for help. And I didn't just ask one person, I asked many. Family and friends were there for me, as I know that family and friends would be for anyone - if the person in need simply asks for help.

This story is meant to serve as a jumping-off point to talk about mental health and to provide one look into the anxiety that some experience. Furthermore, since each person's journey is different, the novel ends with possibility. In no way does the ending mean to suggest that struggles such as these can be easily taken care of with an ice cream, a flower or even a puppy. Still, I wanted to end with some hope for better days - like the ones I am so fortunate enough to experience now.

The subject matter is difficult. Please read with care.

-Jen Degenhardt
July 2023

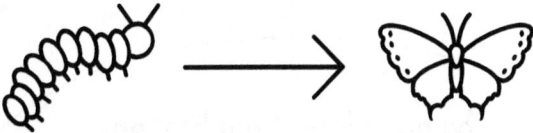

Just when the caterpillar thought the world was over, it became a butterfly...

-proverb

You aren't going to feel this way forever, you know.

The mind has thoughts, and those thoughts control your feelings.

It will all be okay in the end. If it's not okay, it's not the end.

Try to think positively.
Everything in life - including
the bad - is temporary.

I imagine that your path in life
will be a little difficult for a
while, but it won't be forever.
Everything will get better.

Remember: your thoughts
control your feelings. And you
can change your thoughts.

ACKNOWLEDGEMENTS

Having had this story in mind for a while, I started it on the plane on a return flight from California, I think it was. I had done the preparation, taken the notes and had begun writing furiously. And then somehow, I deleted the file. Like, really deleted it, not just in file purgatory. Ugh.

But I had already hired the artist. Juliet Chattaway was still in elementary school when I asked her to draw a teenager in a hoodie, in a bedroom with one window. I then asked her to alter the drawings a bit at a time (I don't want to give it away!), so they too, could be part of the story. Juliet understood my vision exactly, even when I might not always have been so clear. It is a pleasure and an honor to work with student artists like Juliet. They are offered a unique opportunity, and I get to help them realize that "business" doesn't have to be scary. It's a win-win. Many, many thanks to Juliet for her awesome artwork, but also for her patience. Due to - well, life - this novel took longer than I anticipated to get published. Thank you, Juliet!

For this version of the story, I also need to thank Vicki Schrader, an ELL teacher, English grammar guru and a newly minted author in her own right, who helped me with my own Spanish-to-English translation fixing (it's harder than it seems!). I'm grateful for the help.

I owe the following people a huge debt of gratitude (and if you're reading this, or any of my books, so do you. 😊) If not for these people to whom I reached out for help those few years ago, I may not have had the opportunity to write this story - or any others for that matter. I am grateful to each of you. Thank you.

Sarah Jessup & Robert Allen
Celia Bartholomew & John Bartholomew
Angela Degenhardt
Claire Degrigrio
Tara Allen & José Salazar
Amy Salvin Collins
Wendy Perrotti
Patti Nietsch
Rudy Spannaus

In a house...

or an apartment...

or a condominium...

The aunt knocks on the door.

4

The aunt opens the door a little. Ari is on the floor in a dark bedroom, close to the bed.

The aunt opens the door a little more.

Let me raise the shade for the sun to come in.

No, Auntie. I prefer to be in the dark.

21

See you later,
Auntie.

OK. It's only an hour. My aunt trusts me. She says everything is going to be okay, that I'm not going to feel this way forever. But I don't know...

No. It wasn't my fault.
I didn't do anything wrong.

But I didn't ask for such expensive training. I would have preferred to train at a lower level...

No! It's not my fault. But yes, I wanted to keep going in my sport. I really liked winning. And I was winning. I liked when everyone watched me win.

I wasn't the one who took the money from the client. My dad did that. And he said that he wanted to return it...

42

43

45

Ari starts to cry.

51

59

61

Don't blame me. You're not real. I'm the one who's in control...

65

67

My poor dad! He's in prison. And my mom...

72

I need to take it sometimes. It helps me.

So, you don't deny that your present situation is your fault; that if you hadn't participated in that sport, your father wouldn't have stolen that money, and he wouldn't have been arrested and sent to prison. And your mother wouldn't have traveled down that path of destruction.

You don't deny any of that?

It will be better if you take the pills. But, you don't have the guts to hurt yourself. You can't do it...

Ari cries.

Ari picks up the bottle of pills. The only thing that can be heard are the sobs - the sobs of a person in so much pain. She doesn't have any more strength...

Ari is holding the bottle of pills when she slumps over.

A lot of time passes.

The aunt arrives home with a box in her hands.

She doesn't get an answer. The only thing that can be heard are the yips and noises from the puppy in the box.

woof! woof!

The aunt goes to Ari's bedroom. Ari is on the floor with the pill bottle nearby.

The aunt puts down the box
with the puppy and runs to
where Ari is.

Ari's eyes open a little.

96

No, Auntie. I didn't take them

Auntie, I feel awful. I feel guilty. I feel like everything that happened was because...

But he only stole from his client to pay for my training. And because of that crime, my mom drank more and more...

Your parents' decisions were theirs. They are adults. You are not an adult.

Right then, the puppy starts barking again.

What is that, Auntie?

When I was young,
I had a dog called
Shine, Sunshine.

The aunt brings over the box and opens it. The puppy jumps out and goes directly to Ari.

Auntie, thank you! She is super cute and adorable.

Auntie, thank you. Thank you for the support and understanding.

Ari, I imagine that the road ahead is going to be a little difficult for some time, but it won't be forever.

That's a good idea, Auntie

Athena, are you ready?
Let's go.

Hey there!
If you need help, or a
friend needs help, tell
someone. Find a trusted adult
who can help, too. And, check
out the resources below.
☮❤😊

**Suicide and Crisis Lifeline
988 – via phone or text**

**The Crisis Text Line
Text TALK to 741741**

**The American Foundation for
Suicide Prevention
https://afsp.org/get-help**

**Outside of the USA
Find a Helpline
https://findahelpline.com/i/iasp**

127

ABOUT THE AUTHOR

Jennifer Degenhardt taught high school Spanish for over 20 years and now teaches at the college level. At the time she realized her own high school students, many of whom had learning challenges, acquired language best through stories, so she began to write ones that she thought would appeal to them. She has been writing ever since.

Other titles by Jen Degenhardt:

La chica nueva | *La Nouvelle Fille* | <u>The New Girl</u> | *Das Neue Mädchen* | *La nuova ragazza*

La chica nueva (the ancillary/workbook
volume, Kindle book, audiobook)
Salida 8 / Sortie no. 8
Chuchotenango / La terre des chiens errants / La vita dei cani
Pesas / Poids et haltères /Weights and Dumbbells /Pesi
Luis, un soñador
El jersey / The Jersey / Le Maillot
La mochila /The Backpack / Le sac à dos
Moviendo montañas / Déplacer les montagnes /Moving
Mountains / Spostando montagne
La vida es complicada / La vie est compliquée/ Life is
Complicated
La vida es complicada Practice & Questions (workbook)
El Mundial / La Coupe du Monde / The World Cup
Quince /Fifteen / Douze ans
Quince Practice & Questions (workbook)
El viaje difícil/ Un voyage difficile / A Difficult Journey
La niñera
¡¿Fútbol...americano?!/ Football...américain ?!
Era una chica nueva
Levantando pesas: un cuento en el pasado
Se movieron las montañas
Fue un viaje difícil
¿Qué pasó con el jersey?
Cuando se perdió la mochila
Con (un poco de) ayuda de mis amigos /With (a little) Help from
My Friends / Un petit coup de main amical

Con (un po') d'aiuto dai miei amici
La última prueba | The Last Test
Los tres amigos | Three Friends | *Drei Freunde* | *Les trois amis*
La evolución musical
María María: un cuento de un huracán | María María: A Story
of a Story | *Maria Maria: un histoire d'un orage*
Debido a la tormenta | Because of the Storm
La lucha de la vida | The Fight of His Life
Secretos | *Secrets*
Como vuela la pelota
Cambios | *Changements* | Changes
De la oscuridad a la luz
El pueblo | The Town

@JenniferDegenhl

@jendegenhardt9

@PuentesLanguage &
World Language Teaching Stories (group)

Visit www.puenteslanguage.com to sign up to receive
information on new releases and other events.

Check out all titles as ebooks with audio on www.digilangua.net.

141

ABOUT THE ILLUSTRATOR

Juliet Chattaway is a sixth-grade student at New Canaan Country School. She has loved art all her life and draws after school every day. In addition to drawing, Juliet spends her free time reading and writing short stories. One day, she hopes to publish her own Webtoon or book. Juliet lives in Darien, CT with her mother, father and younger brother, Nicholas.